WEALTH WISDOM

Your Guide To Financial Independence And Prosperity

Catherine Moore

Copyright © 2024 Catherine Moore

All rights reserved. No part of this publication may be reproduced, or transmitted in any form or by any means, electronic or mechanical including photocopying, recording or by any information storage and retrieval system without permission in writing from the author

TABLE OF CONTENTS

INTRODUCTION 6
CHAPTER ONE 10
    Money Mind-set Mastery 10
    Transforming Your Financial Attitude 10
    Overcoming Wealth Barriers 12
CHAPTER TWO 16
    The Art of Budgeting 16
    Crafting a Winning Budget 16
    Expense Tracking for Smart Spending 18
CHAPTER THREE 22
    Saving Strategies For Success 22
    Building an Unshakable Emergency Fund 22
    Harnessing the Magic of Compound Interest 24
CHAPTER FOUR 28
    Investing 101: Starting Strong 28
    Navigating Stocks, Bonds, and Mutual Funds 28
    Balancing Risk and Reward 29
CHAPTER FIVE 31
    Advanced Investing: Beyond The Basics 32
    Profiting from Real Estate 32
    Mastering Diversification and Portfolio Management 34
CHAPTER SIX 36

Passive Income Pathways 36
CHAPTER SEVEN 40
    Tax Savvy: Maximizing Returns 40
    Tax-Efficient Investment Strategies 40
    Essential Deductions and Credits 41
CHAPTER EIGHT 44
    Blueprint For Retirement 44
CHAPTER NINE 48
    Estate Planning Essentials 48
    Protecting Your Legacy 49
    Building a Financial Legacy That Lasts 49
CHAPTER TEN 52
    Freedom From Financial Burdens 52
    Accelerating Debt Repayment 53
CHAPTER ELEVEN 54
    Tech-Savvy Financial Tools 54
    Investing Apps 55
    Leveraging Technology for Financial Organization 57
CHAPTER TWELVE 60
    Wealth Protection Tactics 60
    Guarding Against Financial Fraud 62
CHAPTER THIRTEEN 66
    The Joy Of Giving 66
    Charitable Giving Strategies 67

CHAPTER FOURTEEN 70
　The Wealthy Lifestyle 70
CONCLUSION 76

INTRODUCTION

Imagine standing at the crossroads of your financial journey, where every path ahead seems foggy and uncertain. You've heard the stories of those who've achieved financial independence and prosperity, yet for you, it feels like a distant dream. What if I told you that within these pages lies the map to your financial freedom—a guide that will not only illuminate your path but also empower you to master the art of wealth?

Welcome to "Wealth Wisdom: Your Guide to Financial Independence and Prosperity."

This book is not just another financial guide; it's your ultimate companion on the road to financial success. Here, you'll find the keys to unlocking the wealth wisdom you need to transform your financial life. Whether you're overwhelmed by debt, struggling to save, or unsure how to invest, this guide will equip you with the knowledge and tools to overcome every obstacle.

Picture yourself a few months from now: confident, financially savvy, and on a clear path to prosperity. You'll have reshaped your money mind-set, mastered the art of budgeting, and discovered the magic of saving and investing. You'll learn to navigate the complexities of taxes, plan for a comfortable retirement, and build a lasting legacy.

But this journey isn't just about accumulating wealth—it's about achieving a balance that brings peace and fulfilment to your life. As you turn each page, you'll find practical strategies, actionable advice, and inspirational insights designed to help you not just survive, but thrive.

In "Wealth Wisdom," we start by transforming your mind-set, laying a solid foundation for your financial future. You'll learn to see money as a powerful tool, not a source of stress. From there, we'll delve into the essentials of budgeting, saving, and investing, providing you with a comprehensive roadmap to financial independence.

We also explore advanced strategies for maximizing your wealth, including savvy tax planning, retirement preparation, and estate management. Along the way, you'll discover the importance of diversifying your income streams and protecting your wealth from unforeseen challenges.

As you embark on this journey, remember that "Wealth Wisdom" is more than a book—it's your trusted mentor, guiding you every step of the way. Together, we will unlock the secrets to a life of abundance, peace, and prosperity.

Prepare to transform your financial future. Welcome to your guide to financial independence and prosperity. Welcome to "Wealth Wisdom."

CHAPTER ONE

Money Mind-set Mastery

Achieving financial independence and prosperity starts with a crucial first step: mastering your money mind-set. Your financial attitude is the foundation upon which all other financial strategies are built. Without the right mind-set, even the best financial plans can falter. Your attitude towards money—how you think about it, feel about it, and relate to it—forms the bedrock of your financial journey

Transforming Your Financial Attitude

Transforming your financial attitude begins with introspection and a willingness to challenge existing beliefs. Often, we inherit attitudes towards money from our upbringing or societal norms, which may include limiting beliefs such as "money is scarce" or "rich people are greedy." These beliefs can subtly influence our financial decisions and behaviours, holding us back from achieving our true potential.

To transform your financial attitude, start by identifying these limiting beliefs. Question their validity and consider alternative perspectives. Embrace an abundance mind-set, which focuses on opportunities rather than limitations. Understand that wealth is not just about material possessions but also about creating value, achieving goals, and making a positive impact.

Setting clear financial goals is crucial in cultivating a proactive financial attitude. Define what financial success means to you—whether it's achieving financial freedom, funding your children's education, or travelling the world in retirement. Objectives give guidance and inspiration, directing your monetary choices and activities.

Education plays a pivotal role in transforming your financial attitude. Continuously educate yourself about personal finance principles, investment strategies, and economic trends. Knowledge empowers you to make informed decisions and navigate financial challenges with confidence.

Lastly, cultivate gratitude and generosity in your financial mind-set. Appreciate what you have and practice generosity towards others. Viewing money as a tool for positive change fosters a healthier relationship with wealth and enhances your overall well-being.

Overcoming Wealth Barriers

Alongside transforming your financial attitude, overcoming wealth barriers is essential for achieving long-term financial success. These barriers may include internal challenges such as fear of failure, lack of financial literacy, and procrastination, as well as external challenges like debt, living beyond your means, and negative influences.

Fear of failure often paralyzes individuals from taking necessary financial risks. Embrace failure as a stepping stone to learning and growth. Understand that setbacks are temporary and can provide valuable lessons for future success.

A lack of financial literacy can hinder effective financial decision-making. Take proactive steps to enhance your financial knowledge through books, courses, and seminars. Educate yourself on budgeting, saving, investing, and managing debt to build a solid foundation for financial security.

Procrastination is another common barrier to wealth accumulation. Overcome procrastination by breaking down financial goals into manageable steps and taking consistent action towards achieving them. Start small and gradually increase your financial discipline and commitment.

Debt, particularly high-interest debt, can weigh heavily on financial progress. Develop a repayment plan to systematically reduce and eliminate debt. Prioritize paying off debts with the highest interest rates first while maintaining minimum payments on other obligations.

Living beyond your means perpetuates a cycle of financial instability. Practice mindful spending by creating and sticking to a budget that aligns with your financial goals. Differentiate between needs and wants, and prioritize saving and investing for the future.

Be surrounded by positive people who will help you achieve your financial objectives. Minimize exposure to negative influences that encourage unhealthy financial habits or undermine your progress towards financial independence.

Ultimately, mastering your money mind-set requires a commitment to personal growth, continuous learning, and disciplined action. By transforming your financial attitude and overcoming wealth barriers, you empower yourself to navigate the complexities of financial life with clarity, resilience, and confidence.

Embrace the journey towards financial mastery, knowing that each step brings you closer to achieving your dreams and securing a prosperous future.

CHAPTER TWO

The Art of Budgeting

Budgeting is a fundamental skill that empowers individuals and households to manage their finances effectively, achieve financial goals, and build long-term financial stability. At its core, budgeting involves two essential components: crafting a winning budget and implementing effective expense tracking for smart spending.

Crafting a Winning Budget

Crafting a budget is akin to creating a financial roadmap that guides your income towards achieving your financial objectives. It begins with a comprehensive assessment of your financial situation, encompassing income, expenses, debts, and savings goals.

Start by determining all of your income sources, including salaries, wages, earnings from freelance work, investments, and any other revenue sources. Understanding your total income provides clarity on how much money you have available to allocate towards expenses and savings.

Divide your costs into fixed and variable ones as the next step. Fixed expenses are regular payments that remain consistent month to month, such as rent or mortgage payments, utilities, insurance premiums, and loan repayments. Variable expenses fluctuate based on usage or discretionary spending, such as groceries, dining out, entertainment, and personal care.

Depending on importance and necessity, allocate a portion of your income to each category of expenses. Essential expenses like housing, utilities, and debt payments should be prioritized to ensure they are covered each month. Savings and investments should also be included as essential categories within your budget to foster financial growth and security.

Setting clear financial goals is an integral part of crafting a successful budget. Define short-term goals, such as building an emergency fund or saving for a vacation, as well as long-term goals like retirement planning, purchasing a home, or funding education. Allocate a specific portion of your income towards each goal within your budget to ensure steady progress over time.

Check your budget on a regular basis and make any necessary adjustments to account for changes in income, expenses, or financial objectives. Life circumstances evolve, and financial priorities may shift, requiring flexibility in your budgeting approach. Periodic reassessment allows you to optimize your budget and ensure it remains aligned with your current financial situation and objectives.

Expense Tracking for Smart Spending

Effective expense tracking is essential for maintaining financial discipline and optimizing spending habits within your budget. It involves monitoring and recording all expenditures to gain insight into where your money is being spent and identifying areas where adjustments can be made to enhance financial efficiency.

Start by keeping detailed records of your expenses, either manually in a notebook or digitally using budgeting apps or spreadsheets. Categorize expenditures into specific categories such as housing, transportation, food, entertainment, and miscellaneous expenses to facilitate analysis and decision-making.

Compare your actual spending against the budgeted amounts for each category to assess adherence to your financial plan. Identify any discrepancies or overspending in particular areas and evaluate the underlying reasons behind these patterns.

Analyze your spending habits and patterns to identify opportunities for cost savings and optimization. Look for recurring expenses that can be reduced or eliminated, negotiate better deals on regular bills such as utilities or insurance premiums, and consider more economical alternatives for discretionary purchases.

Implement strategies to curb unnecessary spending and maintain financial discipline. Set spending limits for discretionary categories, use cash or debit cards instead of credit cards to avoid accruing debt, and prioritize needs over wants when making purchasing decisions.

Regularly review your expense tracking results to monitor progress towards your financial goals and identify areas for improvement. Celebrate milestones and achievements as you successfully adhere to your budget and make positive changes to your spending habits.

In conclusion, mastering the art of budgeting involves crafting a comprehensive budget that aligns with your financial goals and priorities, and implementing effective expense tracking to monitor spending habits and optimize financial efficiency.

By adopting disciplined budgeting practices, individuals and households can achieve greater financial stability, reduce financial stress, and make informed decisions that support long-term financial well-being. Budgeting is not merely a tool—it is a fundamental skill that empowers individuals to take control of their financial future and achieve their aspirations.

CHAPTER THREE

Saving Strategies For Success

Saving money is not just about setting aside a portion of your income; it's a strategic approach that builds financial security and sets the stage for long-term wealth accumulation. This note explores essential saving strategies, focusing on building an unshakable emergency fund and harnessing the magic of compound interest as key pillars of wealth wisdom.

Building an Unshakable Emergency Fund

An emergency fund is your financial safety net—a reserve of liquid savings that provides peace of mind and protects you from unexpected expenses or financial setbacks. Building and maintaining an adequate emergency fund is crucial for financial stability and resilience.

To get started, decide how much money you want to save for an emergency fund. Means to aggregate something like three to a half year of everyday costs. This fund should cover essential costs such as rent or mortgage payments, utilities, groceries, insurance premiums, and minimum debt payments in case of job loss, illness, or other emergencies.

Allocate a specific portion of your income towards building your emergency fund each month. Treat this savings contribution as a non-negotiable expense, prioritizing it alongside other essential financial obligations. Automate transfers to your savings account to ensure consistency and discipline in saving.

Keep your emergency fund in a separate account that is easily accessible but separate from your regular spending accounts. Opt for a high-yield savings account or a money market account that offers competitive interest rates while maintaining liquidity.

Regularly reassess and replenish your emergency fund as needed. Unexpected costs can arise as life circumstances shift. Periodically review your fund's adequacy and adjust your savings goals or contributions accordingly to ensure you're adequately prepared for unforeseen financial challenges.

Harnessing the Magic of Compound Interest

Compound interest is often hailed as the eighth wonder of the world by Albert Einstein, and for good reason—it has the power to exponentially grow your wealth over time. Understanding and harnessing the magic of compound interest is essential for achieving long-term financial success and building wealth.

Compound interest works by earning interest on both the initial principal and accumulated interest from previous periods. Over time, this compounding effect can significantly increase the value of your investments or savings.

Start early to leverage the full potential of compound interest. The sooner you begin saving and investing, the more time your money has to compound and grow. Even small, regular contributions can snowball into substantial sums over decades, thanks to the power of compounding.

Maximize your savings and investment contributions to take full advantage of compound interest. Contribute consistently to retirement accounts such as 401(k)s or IRAs, where investments can grow tax-deferred or tax-free, depending on the account type and your circumstances.

Reinvest dividends and interest earnings to accelerate the growth of your investments. Instead of withdrawing profits, allow them to compound over time, enhancing the overall return on your investments.

Diversify your investments to mitigate risk while harnessing compound interest. Spread your investments across different asset classes such as stocks, bonds, real estate, and mutual funds to optimize growth potential and protect against market volatility.

Make sure your investments are in line with your financial objectives and risk tolerance by regularly monitoring and reviewing them. Adjust your strategy as needed.

Maintain a disciplined approach to investing and resist the urge to withdraw funds prematurely. The true impact of compound interest is realized over years and decades, making consistency and patience key virtues in wealth accumulation.

Adopting effective saving strategies such as building an unshakable emergency fund and harnessing the magic of compound interest forms the cornerstone of wealth wisdom. These strategies not only safeguard your financial stability in times of uncertainty but also pave the way for long-term wealth accumulation and financial independence.

By prioritizing savings goals, investing wisely, and maintaining discipline, you empower yourself to achieve your financial aspirations and build a secure future. Embrace these strategies as fundamental principles in your journey towards financial success and prosperity.

27 | CATHERINE MOORE

CHAPTER FOUR

Investing 101: Starting Strong

Building wealth and achieving financial goals both require investing. Whether you're just starting or looking to refine your investment strategy, understanding the basics is essential. This note explores key concepts in investing, including navigating stocks, bonds, and mutual funds, and balancing risk and reward.

Navigating Stocks, Bonds, and Mutual Funds

Stocks: Stocks represent ownership in a company and provide the possibility of dividends and capital appreciation. They are considered riskier but can provide higher returns over the long term. When investing in stocks, research companies, assess their financial health and growth prospects, and diversify across different sectors to manage risk.

Bonds: Bonds are obligation protections that enterprises or state-run administrations issue. They provide regular interest payments and a principal return when they reach maturity. Bonds are for the most part thought to be more secure than stocks yet offer lower returns. In a portfolio with a variety of investments, they bring stability and income.

Mutual Funds: Mutual funds pool cash from numerous financial backers to put resources into an expanded arrangement of stocks, bonds, or different resources. They offer diversification and professional management, making them suitable for investors seeking balanced risk exposure. Research fund objectives, fees, and historical performance to select funds aligned with your investment goals.

Balancing Risk and Reward

Risk is the possibility of loss or fluctuation in investment returns. Higher-risk investments like stocks offer greater potential for returns but also carry higher volatility. Lower-risk investments like bonds provide stability but may offer lower returns. Assess your risk tolerance based on financial goals, time horizon, and comfort with market fluctuations.

Risk can be reduced by diversifying your investments across asset classes, industries, and geographic regions. Spread investments to reduce exposure to any single asset or market segment. Diversification can enhance portfolio stability and potential returns by balancing high-risk, high-reward investments with more conservative options.

Allocate assets based on your investment goals, risk tolerance, and time horizon. A balanced portfolio typically includes a mix of stocks, bonds, and other assets tailored to your financial objectives. Adjust asset allocation over time to align with changing goals and market conditions.

Maintain a disciplined approach and avoid making emotional investment decisions based on short-term market fluctuations. Invest for the long term to benefit from compounding returns and weather market cycles. Check and rebalance your portfolio on a regular basis to make sure it stays in line with your goals and investment strategy.

Investing 101 emphasizes starting strong by understanding key investment vehicles like stocks, bonds, and mutual funds, and mastering the art of balancing risk and reward.

By diversifying investments, managing risk effectively, and maintaining a long-term perspective, you can build a resilient investment portfolio that supports your financial aspirations and withstands market fluctuations. Begin your investment journey with knowledge, research, and a clear strategy to achieve financial success and security over the long term.

CHAPTER FIVE

Advanced Investing: Beyond The Basics

Moving beyond the fundamentals of investing opens up a realm of opportunities to strategically grow wealth and achieve financial independence. This chapter explores two advanced strategies—profiting from real estate and mastering diversification and portfolio management—that can elevate your investment approach and propel you towards your financial goals.

Profiting from Real Estate

Real estate investment offers a tangible and potentially lucrative avenue for building wealth over the long term. Unlike stocks or bonds, real estate investments provide opportunities for rental income, property appreciation, and tax benefits. Here's how to capitalize on real estate investment:

Conduct thorough research and due diligence when selecting investment properties. Consider factors such as location, market trends, rental demand, and potential for appreciation. Diversify your real estate holdings across different property types and geographic areas to spread risk and optimize returns.

Generate steady cash flow by renting out investment properties. Calculate rental yields and ensure they cover expenses such as mortgage payments, property taxes, insurance, and maintenance costs. Aim for properties with strong rental potential and consider property management services to streamline operations.

Real estate investments can appreciate over time, increasing your overall wealth. Monitor market conditions and economic trends to capitalize on opportunities for property value growth. Leverage mortgage financing wisely to amplify returns while managing leverage risks effectively.

Explore tax benefits associated with real estate investing, such as deductions for mortgage interest, property depreciation, and operating expenses. Consult with a tax advisor to maximize tax advantages and optimize your investment strategy.

Mastering Diversification and Portfolio Management

Diversification is a fundamental strategy that involves spreading investments across different asset classes, industries, and geographic regions to reduce risk and optimize returns. Effective portfolio management enhances diversification while aligning investments with your financial goals:

Determine an appropriate asset allocation based on your risk tolerance, investment horizon, and financial objectives. Allocate investments among stocks, bonds, real estate, and other asset classes to achieve a balanced portfolio. Rebalance periodically to maintain desired asset allocation and adjust for market fluctuations.

Mitigate portfolio risk through diversification and asset allocation. Monitor investment performance and adjust holdings as needed to align with changing market conditions and economic outlooks. Consider hedging strategies, such as options or futures contracts, to protect against downside risk in volatile markets.

Regularly review your investment portfolio's performance and progress towards financial goals. Evaluate individual investment holdings, assess their contribution to overall portfolio returns, and make informed decisions based on thorough analysis and market insights.

Adopt a disciplined and patient approach to investing. Focus on long-term wealth accumulation and resist the urge to react impulsively to short-term market fluctuations. Stay committed to your investment strategy and adjust it strategically as your financial circumstances and objectives evolve.

In conclusion, advanced investing goes beyond the basics by leveraging opportunities in real estate and mastering diversification and portfolio management. By strategically investing in real estate for income and appreciation, and optimizing portfolio diversification and risk management techniques, you can enhance your investment strategy and accelerate progress towards financial independence. Embrace these advanced strategies with knowledge, diligence, and a long-term perspective to unlock greater potential for wealth accumulation and achieve your financial aspirations.

CHAPTER SIX

Passive Income Pathways

Passive income represents more than just financial security—it embodies the freedom to shape a lifestyle where earning potential isn't limited by time or location. By strategically diversifying income sources and harnessing personal passions, individuals can cultivate a sustainable path towards financial independence.

Creating Multiple Streams of Income:

Diversifying income sources is a cornerstone of financial resilience. By spreading investments across different asset classes, individuals can mitigate risk and optimize returns. Stocks, for example, offer opportunities for capital appreciation and dividend income, while bonds provide steady interest payments with lower volatility. Real estate investments can yield rental income and potential property appreciation, serving as a stable income stream over time.

Additionally, ventures into entrepreneurial endeavours such as online businesses or peer-to-peer lending platforms offer avenues for generating supplementary income, leveraging individual skills and market opportunities.

The key to creating multiple streams of income lies in strategic asset allocation and diversification. Each income stream contributes to a more robust financial portfolio, enhancing overall stability and resilience against economic fluctuations.

Moreover, the passive nature of these income streams allows individuals to earn money without being tied to a specific location or working full-time hours, opening up opportunities for greater personal freedom and flexibility.

Monetizing Your Passions:

Transforming hobbies or specialized skills into revenue streams not only enhances financial well-being but also fosters personal fulfilment. Freelancing or consulting services allow individuals to leverage expertise in areas like marketing, design, or coaching, providing flexible income opportunities.

Content creation through blogs, podcasts, or digital courses monetizes knowledge and creativity, reaching global audiences through advertising, sponsorships, or paid subscriptions. Licensing intellectual property or franchising successful business models further expands income potential while leveraging existing assets and market demand.

By embracing diverse passive income strategies and nurturing personal interests, individuals cultivate resilience against economic uncertainty while enjoying the autonomy to pursue meaningful endeavours.

The pursuit of passive income is not just about financial gain; it's about designing a life where work aligns with passion and purpose, fostering sustained fulfilment and long-term prosperity. Start exploring these pathways today to build a more secure and abundant future, where financial freedom becomes a tangible reality.

CHAPTER SEVEN

Tax Savvy: Maximizing Returns

As Understanding the intricacies of taxation is crucial for optimizing your financial returns and securing a stronger financial future. By implementing tax-efficient investment strategies and capitalizing on essential deductions and credits, you can effectively minimize tax liabilities and retain more of your income.

Tax-Efficient Investment Strategies

Investing strategically can significantly impact your tax obligations. One effective strategy is to utilize retirement accounts such as IRAs and 401(k)s, which offer tax advantages like tax-deferred growth or tax-free withdrawals in the case of Roth accounts. By contributing to these accounts, you not only save for retirement but also reduce your taxable income in the current year.

Diversifying your investments across asset classes can also play a role in tax efficiency. For instance, municipal bonds provide interest income that is typically exempt from federal taxes and sometimes state taxes, making them attractive for investors in higher tax brackets.

There are a number of tax advantages to investing in real estate, such as the ability to deduct mortgage interest, property taxes, and depreciation. These deductions can offset rental income and reduce taxable income, while property appreciation adds to long-term wealth accumulation.

Essential Deductions and Credits

Maximizing deductions is essential for lowering your taxable income. Itemizing deductions allows you to deduct expenses such as mortgage interest, state and local taxes, charitable donations, and medical expenses that exceed a certain threshold. This approach is beneficial if your total deductible expenses exceed the standard deduction amount.

Your tax burden is reduced in proportion to the amount of tax credits you receive. For example, educational credits like the American Opportunity Tax Credit (AOTC) and

Lifetime Learning Credit (LLC) can offset the costs of higher education expenses for yourself, your spouse, or your dependents, thereby lowering your tax liability.

Health-related expenses can also be tax deductible. Contributions to Health Savings Accounts (HSAs) are tax-deductible, and withdrawals for qualified medical expenses are tax-free. This dual tax benefit makes HSAs a powerful tool for managing healthcare costs while reducing taxable income.

For small business owners and self-employed individuals, deductions for business expenses, depreciation of assets, and contributions to retirement plans such as SEP-IRAs or Solo 401(k)s can effectively lower taxable income. These deductions not only reduce immediate tax liabilities but also facilitate long-term savings and investment growth.

By integrating these tax-efficient strategies and maximizing deductions and credits, you can optimize your overall tax position and enhance your after-tax returns.

It's essential to stay informed about changes in tax laws and consult with a tax advisor to tailor strategies to your specific financial circumstances. Taking a proactive approach to tax planning ensures that you make informed decisions that align with your financial goals and aspirations.

CHAPTER EIGHT

Blueprint For Retirement

Retirement planning is a crucial aspect of financial preparedness, ensuring a secure and enjoyable post-career life. Understanding the intricacies of retirement accounts such as 401(k)s, IRAs, and Roth IRAs is essential for crafting a robust blueprint towards a golden retirement.

Understanding 401(k)s:

A 401(k) is an employer-sponsored retirement plan that allows employees to contribute a portion of their pre-tax income towards retirement savings. These contributions are tax-deferred, meaning you do not pay taxes on the money until you withdraw it during retirement.

Contributions that are matched by many employers can significantly boost your retirement savings. Your taxable income is reduced in the year you make contributions to a traditional 401(k), resulting in immediate tax advantages.

Understanding IRAs:

Personal retirement savings accounts known as Individual Retirement Accounts (IRAs) provide tax advantages. Traditional IRAs allow you to make tax-deductible contributions, which grow tax-deferred until withdrawal in retirement. Roth IRAs, on the other hand, are funded with after-tax dollars, but withdrawals in retirement are tax-free, including any earnings on your investments, provided certain conditions are met. IRAs offer flexibility in investment choices, including stocks, bonds, mutual funds, and more.

Planning for a Golden Retirement:

Planning for retirement involves setting realistic financial goals, estimating future expenses, and creating a savings strategy that aligns with your desired lifestyle. Begin by calculating your retirement needs based on expected expenses, including housing, healthcare, and leisure activities. Consider factors like inflation and potential healthcare costs in your planning.

Diversifying your retirement savings across different accounts, such as 401(k)s, IRAs, and Roth IRAs, helps manage tax implications and provides flexibility in accessing funds during retirement. Regularly review and adjust your retirement plan as your circumstances change, and stay informed about updates to tax laws and retirement account rules.

By understanding the nuances of retirement accounts and taking a proactive approach to retirement planning, you can build a solid foundation for a golden retirement. Seek guidance from financial advisors or retirement planning professionals to tailor a retirement blueprint that suits your unique financial situation and aspirations. Start planning early to maximize your retirement savings and enjoy a fulfilling and financially secure future.

CHAPTER NINE

Estate Planning Essentials

Estate planning is a vital process that ensures your assets are distributed according to your wishes and your loved ones are protected after you pass away. Understanding the essentials of estate planning—wills, trusts, and building a lasting financial legacy—is crucial for securing your family's future.

Wills and Trusts:

A will is an authoritative record that determines your desires in regard to the dissemination of your property and resources upon your passing. It lets you name beneficiaries for specific assets and a person to act on your behalf as executor. Wills can also address guardianship for minor children and specify funeral arrangements.

On the other hand, trusts are legal structures that hold assets for beneficiaries. They can be revocable or irrevocable and serve various purposes such as minimizing estate taxes, avoiding probate, and providing ongoing financial management for beneficiaries. Trusts offer flexibility in distributing assets according to specific conditions you set.

Protecting Your Legacy

Estate planning goes beyond distributing assets—it encompasses protecting your legacy and ensuring your wishes are honoured. Consider establishing powers of attorney to designate someone to make financial or medical decisions on your behalf if you become incapacitated. Healthcare directives outline your preferences for medical treatment in case you are unable to communicate them yourself.

Life insurance is another essential component of estate planning, providing financial security to your loved ones after your death. It can replace lost income, cover outstanding debts, or fund expenses such as college tuition for your children.

Building a Financial Legacy That Lasts

Building a lasting financial legacy involves more than passing on assets—it means imparting values, wisdom, and financial responsibility to future generations. Consider educating heirs about money management and creating a plan for transferring wealth efficiently. Charitable giving through trusts or foundations can also be part of your legacy, allowing you to support causes that are important to you beyond your lifetime.

Regularly review and update your estate plan to reflect changes in your family dynamics, financial situation, or estate laws. Consult with estate planning professionals, such as attorneys or financial advisors, to ensure your plan is comprehensive and legally sound.

By understanding estate planning essentials and taking proactive steps to protect and build your legacy, you can secure your family's financial future and leave a meaningful impact for generations to come. Start planning today to safeguard your assets and ensure your wishes are fulfilled with care and foresight.

CHAPTER TEN

Freedom From Financial Burdens

Achieving financial freedom involves understanding the nature of debt and implementing strategies to manage and eliminate it effectively. By distinguishing between good and bad debt and accelerating debt repayment, individuals can lighten their financial burdens and pave the way towards a more secure future.

Identifying Good vs. Bad Debt:

Good debt typically refers to loans or investments that can potentially increase your net worth or generate income over time. For example, student loans can lead to higher earning potential through education, while a mortgage allows you to build equity in a home. These debts are considered investments in your future financial well-being.

On the other hand, bad debt typically includes high-interest consumer debt used to finance depreciating assets or non-essential expenses. Credit card debt, payday loans, or car loans with high interest rates fall into this category. Such debts can hinder financial progress and lead to long-term financial strain if not managed carefully.

Accelerating Debt Repayment

Accelerating debt repayment involves prioritizing debt elimination by allocating additional funds towards paying off outstanding balances. Start by creating a budget that identifies discretionary income available for debt repayment. Consider employing debt repayment strategies such as the debt snowball method (paying off debts from smallest to largest balance) or the debt avalanche method (paying off debts with the highest interest rates first).

Increasing income through side gigs or freelance work can provide extra funds to accelerate debt repayment. Negotiating lower interest rates or consolidating high-interest debts into lower-interest loans can also facilitate faster debt payoff.

By focusing on identifying and managing good vs. bad debt and implementing strategies to accelerate debt repayment, individuals can regain financial freedom and reduce stress associated with debt. Establishing sound financial habits, such as budgeting and disciplined spending, is essential.

CHAPTER ELEVEN

Tech-Savvy Financial Tools

In the digital age, managing finances has become more accessible and efficient thanks to a variety of apps designed for budgeting and investing. Leveraging these technological tools can help you organize your finances, track spending, save money, and grow your investments with ease.

Budgeting Apps

Mint: Mint is one of the most popular budgeting apps, offering a comprehensive suite of tools to track your spending, create budgets, and set financial goals. It links to your bank accounts, credit cards, and bills, providing an up-to-date overview of your financial situation. With customizable alerts for bill payments and budget limits, Mint helps you stay on top of your finances effortlessly.

YNAB (You Need A Budget): YNAB is a proactive budgeting app that encourages users to allocate every dollar they earn to specific expenses or savings. The app's methodology is based on four simple rules: Give every dollar a job, embrace your true expenses, roll with the punches, and age your money. YNAB offers detailed reports and educational resources, making it a robust tool for those committed to gaining control over their finances.

Pocket Guard: Pocket Guard helps you track your income, bills, and expenses to show how much disposable income you have. It's ideal for people who want a clear picture of their financial situation at a glance. The app automatically categorizes expenses, identifies areas where you can save, and even negotiates lower bills on your behalf.

Investing Apps

Robinhood: Robinhood revolutionized investing by offering commission-free trades of stocks, ETFs, and crypto currencies. The app is user-friendly, making it accessible for beginners while also providing advanced tools for more experienced investors. Robinhood's cash management feature allows users to earn interest on uninvested cash, further optimizing their financial strategy.

Acorns: Acorns simplifies investing by rounding up your everyday purchases to the nearest dollar and investing the spare change in a diversified portfolio. This micro-investing approach makes it easy for beginners to start investing without needing a large sum of money. Acorns also offers retirement accounts and educational content to help users make informed decisions.

Betterment: Betterment is a robo-advisor that provides personalized investment advice based on your financial goals. It offers automated portfolio management, tax-efficient strategies, and financial planning tools. Betterment's intuitive interface and low fees make it a great option for those looking to optimize their investments with minimal effort.

Wealth front: Wealthfront is another leading robo-advisor that offers comprehensive financial planning and investment management services. It uses sophisticated algorithms to create and manage a diversified portfolio tailored to your risk tolerance and goals. Wealthfront also provides banking services, such as high-interest savings accounts and automated financial planning.

Leveraging Technology for Financial Organization

Utilizing these budgeting and investing apps can significantly enhance your financial organization. By consolidating your financial information in one place, you gain a clearer understanding of your income, expenses, and investment performance. These apps provide tools for setting and tracking financial goals, helping you stay accountable and make informed decisions.

Moreover, the automation features offered by many of these apps—such as automatic transaction categorization, investment rebalancing, and personalized financial advice—save time and reduce the cognitive load associated with managing finances. This allows you to focus on achieving your financial goals rather than getting bogged down by the minutiae of financial management.

Leveraging technology through budgeting and investing apps empowers you to take control of your financial future with greater ease and confidence. Whether you're looking to better manage your day-to-day expenses or grow your wealth through smart investments, there's an app designed to meet your needs and simplify your financial journey.

CHAPTER TWELVE

Wealth Protection Tactics

Protecting your wealth is as crucial as accumulating it. Effective wealth protection involves understanding and utilizing insurance to safeguard your assets, as well as implementing strategies to guard against financial fraud. Here's an in-depth look at these two essential aspects of wealth protection.

Insurance Basics You Need to Know

Insurance is a fundamental tool in protecting your financial well-being. It provides a safety net that can help cover unexpected costs, thereby preserving your wealth.

Health Insurance: This is perhaps the most critical form of insurance, as medical expenses can be substantial and unexpected. Health insurance helps cover the costs of doctor visits, hospital stays, medications, and preventive care. Without it, a significant health issue could deplete your savings.

Life Insurance: If you pass away, life insurance helps your heirs pay for funeral expenses. It can help cover living expenses, pay off debts, and ensure your family's financial stability. There are two main types: term life insurance, which provides coverage for a specified period, and whole life insurance, which offers lifelong coverage and includes a savings component.

Homeowners or Renters Insurance: Homeowners insurance protects your home and belongings against damage or loss from events like fire, theft, or natural disasters. Renters insurance covers your personal property within a rented residence. Both types of insurance can also provide liability coverage if someone is injured on your property.

Auto Insurance: Auto insurance is essential for covering costs related to car accidents, including vehicle repairs, medical expenses, and liability for damages. It is mandatory in most states and ensures that you are financially protected in the event of an accident.

Disability Insurance: This type of insurance provides income replacement if you are unable to work due to illness or injury. Short-term disability insurance covers temporary conditions, while long-term disability insurance provides benefits for extended periods or permanent disabilities.

Umbrella Insurance: Umbrella insurance offers additional liability coverage beyond what is provided by your other insurance policies. It protects your assets from major claims and lawsuits, ensuring that your wealth is not jeopardized by unforeseen legal issues.

Guarding Against Financial Fraud

In addition to having adequate insurance, safeguarding your wealth also involves protecting yourself against financial fraud. Here are some strategies to help you guard against fraud:

Check your bank and credit card statements frequently to look for unauthorized transactions. Set up cautions to inform you of any surprising movement. Inform your financial institution of any discrepancies as soon as possible.

Safeguard Individual Data: Be wary of your own data. Shred delicate reports, serious areas of strength for utilize, passwords for online records, and try not to share individual subtleties via telephone or through unstable sites. Phishing scams, which frequently involve forged emails or messages intended to steal your information, should be avoided.

Use Secure Payment Methods: When shopping online, ensure that the website is secure (look for "https" in the URL). When making online purchases, use credit cards rather than debit cards because credit cards are more resistant to fraud. Consider using digital wallets or payment services that provide an extra layer of security.

Be Cautious with Investments: Research investment opportunities thoroughly before committing your money. Be wary of "too good to be true" offers, high-pressure sales tactics, or unsolicited investment advice. Work with reputable financial advisors and institutions.

Stay Informed: Educate yourself about common types of financial fraud and stay updated on new scams. The more you know, the better equipped you are to recognize and avoid fraudulent schemes.

By understanding and utilizing insurance effectively, you can protect your wealth from unforeseen events. Simultaneously, by implementing strategies to guard against financial fraud, you can ensure that your hard-earned money remains secure. Together, these tactics form a robust defence against the myriad risks that can threaten your financial well-being.

CHAPTER THIRTEEN

The Joy Of Giving

True wealth is not only measured by the amount of money you accumulate but also by the positive impact you can make with it. The joy of giving is an enriching aspect of financial success, allowing you to support causes that matter to you and make a lasting difference in the lives of others. Understanding how to make an impact with your wealth and employing effective charitable giving strategies can maximize the benefits of your philanthropy.

Making an Impact with Your Wealth

Giving back to society can be one of the most fulfilling aspects of financial success. Whether you support educational initiatives, healthcare, environmental conservation, or social justice causes, your contributions can drive meaningful change. The key to making a significant impact is to align your giving with your values and passions. Identify the issues that resonate with you personally and consider how your resources can address these challenges.

Research organizations and causes thoroughly to ensure that your donations are used effectively. Look for charities with transparent operations and measurable outcomes. By investing in organizations with a proven track record, you can be confident that your contributions are making a real difference. Additionally, consider engaging in hands-on philanthropy by volunteering your time and skills, which can amplify the impact of your financial contributions.

Charitable Giving Strategies

Effective charitable giving involves more than just writing a check. There are various strategies you can employ to maximize the impact of your donations while also benefiting from potential tax advantages.

Direct Donations: One of the simplest ways to give is through direct donations to your chosen charities. Cash donations are straightforward and immediately beneficial to the recipient organization. Ensure you keep records of your donations for tax deduction purposes.

Donor-Advised Funds (DAFs): DAFs are philanthropic investment accounts that allow you to donate cash, stocks, or other assets and receive an immediate tax deduction. The funds can then be spread out over time to charities. DAFs offer flexibility, allowing you to invest the funds for growth while deciding which charities to support and when.

Charitable Trusts: Charitable remainder trusts (CRTs) and charitable lead trusts (CLTs) are estate planning tools that allow you to donate assets to a trust, which then provides income to either you (CRTs) or a charity (CLTs) for a specified period. After this period, the remaining assets are transferred to your chosen charity (CRTs) or your beneficiaries (CLTs). These trusts can offer significant tax benefits and help you manage your estate more effectively.

Legacy Giving: Including charitable donations in your will or estate plan ensures that your philanthropic goals are carried out after your lifetime. You can designate specific amounts or a percentage of your estate to be donated to your preferred charities. Legacy giving allows you to leave a lasting impact and support the causes you care about even after you are gone.

Matching Gifts: Many employers offer matching gift programs, where they match the charitable contributions made by their employees. This can double or even triple the impact of your donation. Check with your employer to see if they have a matching gift program and take advantage of this opportunity.

Qualified Charitable Distributions (QCDs): If you are over 70½ years old, you can make tax-free donations directly from your IRA to a qualified charity. QCDs count towards your required minimum distributions (RMDs) but are not included in your taxable income, offering a tax-efficient way to donate.

By employing these charitable giving strategies, you can maximize the impact of your donations, ensuring that your wealth contributes to meaningful and lasting change. The joy of giving comes not only from the act of donating but also from knowing that you are making a difference in the world. Whether through direct donations, donor-advised funds, charitable trusts, or legacy giving, your philanthropy can leave a positive mark on society, reflecting your values and passions for generations to come.

CHAPTER FOURTEEN

The Wealthy Lifestyle

The concept of a wealthy lifestyle often conjures images of opulent mansions, luxury cars, and extravagant vacations. While these symbols of affluence are commonly associated with wealth, the true essence of a wealthy lifestyle extends far beyond material possessions. It encompasses a holistic approach to living that prioritizes well-being, fulfilment, and a sense of purpose.

Financial Freedom: The Foundation of Wealth

Financial freedom is the cornerstone of a wealthy lifestyle. It's not just about amassing riches, but about having the means to live life on your own terms. You are able to make decisions based on desire rather than necessity when you have financial freedom. This freedom is achieved through smart financial planning, wise investments, and disciplined spending. It's about creating a sustainable wealth that supports your dreams and ambitions without the constant worry about money.

Time Affluence: The Ultimate Luxury

One of the most coveted aspects of a wealthy lifestyle is time affluence—the luxury of having control over your time. Unlike money, time is a non-renewable resource. Wealth provides the privilege to pursue passions, engage in hobbies, and spend quality time with loved ones. It's about creating a balanced life where work and leisure coexist harmoniously, allowing you to savour each moment and live fully.

Health and Wellness: The True Wealth

Health is often said to be the greatest wealth, and for good reason. A wealthy lifestyle places a high premium on physical and mental well-being. This includes access to nutritious food, regular exercise, and top-notch medical care. Equally important is mental health, nurtured through mindfulness, stress management, and meaningful connections. Prioritizing health ensures that you can enjoy your wealth with vigour and vitality.

Lifelong Learning: Enriching the Mind

A truly wealthy lifestyle is one of perpetual growth and learning. Education, whether through formal means or self-directed exploration, enriches life and opens doors to new opportunities. Continuous learning keeps the mind sharp, fuels curiosity, and fosters personal development. Wealth affords the resources to pursue knowledge and skills that elevate your personal and professional life.

Giving Back: The Joy of Contribution

The positive influence you have on other people determines your true wealth. Philanthropy and community service are integral to a wealthy lifestyle. Giving back not only supports those in need but also brings a profound sense of fulfilment and purpose. It's about using your resources to make the world a better place, creating a legacy of generosity and compassion.

Experiences Over Possessions: Creating Memories

While material possessions provide comfort, it's the experiences that create lasting joy. Travel, cultural activities, and shared moments with loved ones enrich life far beyond the fleeting pleasure of owning things. A wealthy lifestyle values experiences that foster growth, create cherished memories, and deepen connections with others.

Work-Life Balance: Harmony in Living

Achieving a healthy work-life balance is essential to a wealthy lifestyle. It's about finding equilibrium between professional ambitions and personal well-being. This balance allows you to be productive without compromising your health or happiness. A fulfilling career should complement a rich personal life, creating a harmonious existence.

Environmental and Social Responsibility: Conscious Living

A wealthy lifestyle includes a commitment to environmental and social responsibility. It's about making choices that promote sustainability and ethical practices. Whether it's supporting eco-friendly products or advocating for social justice, individuals who lead wealthy lives are mindful of their impact on the world and strive to contribute positively.

The Essence of True Wealth

The wealthy lifestyle is a multifaceted approach to living that goes beyond financial success. It's about cultivating a life rich in experiences, health, learning, and meaningful connections. It's about using your resources to create a positive impact and leaving a legacy that extends beyond material wealth. By embracing these principles, you can achieve a life of true abundance and fulfilment.

CONCLUSION

As we reach the end of Wealth Wisdom: Your Guide to Financial Independence and Prosperity, it's clear that wealth extends far beyond mere numbers in a bank account. True prosperity is about achieving a harmonious balance between financial security, personal fulfilment, and purposeful living.

The strategies and insights shared in this book are designed to empower you to take control of your financial future, making informed decisions that align with your deepest values and aspirations. By mastering the principles of smart investing, disciplined spending, and continuous learning, you pave the way for not only financial independence but a richer, more meaningful life.

Remember, wealth is not just about accumulating money but also about creating a life that reflects your dreams and values. It's about having the freedom to pursue passions, build lasting relationships, and make a positive impact on the world.

As you embark on your journey toward financial independence and prosperity, keep these lessons close to your heart. Let them guide you through challenges and celebrate your successes. Your path to wealth is unique, and with wisdom as your compass, you are equipped to navigate it with confidence and grace. Here's to your prosperous future—one filled with abundance, joy, and purpose.